Everyday

George Guiver is the Vice-Principal of the College of the Resurrection, in Mirfield, West Yorkshire, one of the Church of England's Theological Colleges, and a member of the Community of the Resurrection. He is also the author of *Company of Voices: Daily Prayer and the People of God* (SPCK 1988) and *Faith in Momentum* (SPCK 1990).

EVERYDAY GOD

GEORGE GUIVER CR

✄

Triangle

First published in Great Britain 1994

Triangle
Society for Promoting Christian Knowledge
Holy Trinity Church
Marylebone Road
London NW1 4DU

Author's note
Most of the biblical quotations are translations from combined sources.
Direct use is made of *The New English Bible* (NEB), © 1961, 1970
Oxford and Cambridge University Presses, and *The Revised
Standard Version* (RSV) © 1971 and 1952, as acknowledged in the text.

British Library Cataloguing-in-Publication Data
A catalogue record for this book is available from the British Library

ISBN 0–281–04766–9

Typeset by Dorwyn Ltd, Rowlands Castle, Hants
Printed and bound in Great Britain by
BPC Paperbacks Ltd
Member of The British Printing Company Ltd

Contents

1 *Looking for God*

Where is God? Why is he so silent? Where can we find him?

Many people ask themselves questions like this today. When we are in town shopping or doing errands, everything looks completely ordinary. The people hustling by on the street, the noise of the traffic, bright lights in shop windows full of attractive goods – none of it seems to fit with God. The litter blows about on the pavement as if to say: 'This is all there is.' The newspapers sit in the newsagent's rack – they know what makes the news: international crises, falls in interest rates, business scandals, titbits about the royals. Never, on the other hand, is there a headline about God. People crowd into the newsagent's shop every day, but not many of us will be praying while we wait. We linger in the warm waiting our turn – to one a *Daily Mirror* and a Mars bar, to another Benson and Hedges and the *Independent*. In buses and offices, in factories, in front rooms and kitchens, the daily round follows its course. Some face another day of struggling on. Some will be lonely, some sad, some happy. The typewriter, the workshop, the morning cuppa, the children, the bills, sitting with a meal on our lap watching the news: these are real. God isn't. It takes a great effort to think that God is so real.

Why? Why does ordinary life feel worlds away from the Church and from God?

One answer is: 'Say your prayers – then God will be real to you.' Now that is all very well, but a lot of people have problems with it. All the world over today there are people who say, 'I can't pray'; or they find it really hard going. Some Christians have given up saying their prayers a long time ago, and rely simply on going to church on Sundays. Even many clergy find it difficult to pray. As for prayer in the family, that used to be taken for granted, but it is very rare nowadays. A common scene in cowboy films is the pious American family saying their grace together at table. We have seen something similar in a recent television comedy series about a Roman Catholic family. But to find a Christian family praying together is something hardly known in modern Britain. We find prayer very difficult. Jesus, on the other hand, told us to pray with confidence, and our prayer will be heard by the Father. Why is it then that we often find it so hard? Surely we must be making a mistake somewhere?

There is good news for all of us who try to pray, and especially for those who find it very difficult. This good news is some simple common sense which our forebears used to know, and which we have forgotten. Because we have forgotten it, we are, as the saying goes, up a gum-tree. We need to come down from our tree and rediscover what we have lost. With this common sense our prayer can be transformed, and it can help us to find an answer to our questions: 'Where is God?' 'Where can we find him?'

First of all we need to start with something surprisingly obvious. We think of God as a person, and we expect to be able to talk with God as one person to another. This is how Jesus describes God in the New Testament. For him, God is our father, and we are his sons and daughters. Jesus said 'You are my friends'. Well, if God is like a person, then the way we get on with God will be like the way we get on with David or Joanne or Shirley. The way we get on with them will be able to tell us a lot about how we can start with God. It is very interesting therefore to take a look at how we get on with each other.

Imagine you are going around the corner to the news-agent's. On the way you meet Evelyn. Each of you says, 'Hello'. Evelyn asks how you are, how the family is, and you reply and ask the same questions back. You may then get on to the weather, or perhaps how the sprouts are doing in the garden. Then aches and pains, perhaps. Finally each of you gets a sense that it is time to move on. It is always to some extent a bit of a cat-and-mouse game, as we feel ourselves in this person's presence, and we begin to sense that the point has come where we need to start trying to extricate ourselves. So we work our way towards taking our leave with a few standard phrases and gestures.

A little further down the road you meet somebody else, and the same thing starts all over again. It is a ritual. We address each other in a way which is patterned, structured, put together from a set of bits and pieces. A lot of our conversation with people is just like that: rituals, set ways of saying and doing things. If that is how we get on with each other, then it is difficult to see how we will be able to pray without the same kind of thing. We can only talk to God in ways that we are used to.

Yet we assume that talking with God in prayer is going to be so different, so unique, that we don't know how to go about it. Why should it be so different from the way we talk with people we know? Jesus said, 'I call you my friends' (John 15.15), and he encouraged us to speak to God as we would to our own father or mother. If that is the case, then prayer, which is our conversation with God, will have something in common with the way we talk to people in the street or anywhere else.

So far, we have noticed that the way we greet people can often be a kind of ritual. Now notice another thing. We assume we need to concentrate when we pray. Perhaps we close our eyes firmly, lean forward, and try to concentrate on God with all our might, directing every bit of our attention on him. Now why do we do this? We don't behave like that with other people, so why should we expect to do it with God? When we meet someone in the street, how much do we concentrate on them? Not very much. Imagine talking to Evelyn. All the time that we are talking, other things are on our mind – whether the shop will have run out of bread, what to do about a bust-up in the family, the throbbing of a corn on our left foot. That is how we are made. In fact, if we

4

concentrated on other people with all our attention all the time, if we passionately shook their hand, staring into their eyes, they would probably want to run away as quickly as they could. Why then should we think we have to behave like that when we pray to God? It is unnecessary and unnatural to expect to do that all the time. Certainly, there are times for such concentration, just as there are with people – when we are listening to someone in tears, for example, or questioning someone closely about a sensitive matter, or delighting in one we love. But we don't do that all the time.

If you watch yourself as you live out your life from day to day, you will in fact be surprised to realize that for a lot of the time we relate to each other with varying degrees of vacancy. We can't keep up intense concentration on people for long, except in times of danger, crisis or passion. We are simply not made in a way that can normally sustain great mental concentration on people.

This suggests that for a lot of the time prayer may in fact be fairly relaxed and unconcentrated. As in our dealings with other people, there are times for concentrating, times for wandering with our thoughts, times when we are just vaguely paying attention.

But look at ourselves once we start praying. Someone at a meeting says 'Let us pray', and everyone automatically shuts their eyes tight and hunches up. 'Concentrate hard,' their attitude seems to say. Sometimes this may be right. But it can also be an unnatural thing to do. It might be better to stay upright and relaxed with our eyes open. Why do we think we have to put on this strange act every time? We don't do it with other people – why should we do it with God? It is a habit which we have been taught, perhaps since childhood, without ever stopping to question it.

Anyway, it seems likely from all of this that when we speak with God we shall do it, as we do with Joanne or Robert, in certain set ways, frequently with familiar words, phrases, and gestures, and that we shall often be quite vacant about it. We shall talk to him as we talk to others, thinking off and on about other things at the same time. That is how we are.

We have begun to look at our problems in getting to know God. It involves many things which are quite easy to become familiar with, and over the next few chapters we shall be trying to see what they are.

2 *Getting to know someone*

Getting to know God is like getting to know anybody else. Everyday life with other people can be very helpful in telling us whether we are going about prayer in a sensible way. It takes us years to learn how to relate to others. While we are learning it, as children and as teenagers, and even afterwards, we often misunderstand people, or say the wrong thing. Getting on with God is bound to be very much the same: we can only do what we are used to. If we think knowing God is very different from knowing other people, then we are trying to do something for which we have no equipment and very little natural ability. No wonder many people flounder in prayer, when they are told to go away and do something strange and demanding, like sitting in complete silence, or to do other unusual things which have little connection with their daily experience of life. Prayer *is* different, but not that different.

We mustn't over-simplify. God is not like us, in that we can't offer him a cup of tea, or shake his hand. We can't talk with him and join in activities with him in the same way as with our next-door neighbour or with Aunt Elsie. So we can't claim that prayer to God is exactly like talking with anybody else. And yet there are very many similarities. There have to be, because we can only behave in the way we are made. We make getting to know God too difficult for ourselves. We think God is a kind of invisible gas, and our job is to try and sniff him out. 'If only I could sniff the invisible perfume of God, then I could really believe.' Or we think he is like the waves of Radio One passing invisibly through our room: we need to tune in our personal radio so that we can pick him up. Why is it that the reception is often crackly or feeble? we ask. It is because we have misunderstood. God is not simply invisible. There is more to it than that. Comparisons with everyday life can help to set that right. Relating to God is special, and it makes unusual demands of us. But it is not so different and extraordinary – it is more like everyday life than we realize.

To return to the two people greeting each other in the street – we see they use a lot of standard phrases, and the conversation more often than not follows a fairly standard pattern. Many of the things we say are quite predictable. The better someone knows us, the more they will know what to expect from us. We may know, for instance, just the thing to say to our brother to tease and irritate him – we often have a good idea what response we will get from him. People are often predictable. And the way we get on with each other includes many set ways of doing things which are also fairly predictable. It has to be the same with God, for he encourages us to relate to him as one human being does to another.

Notice also that the less well we know somebody the more formally we speak to them. Even when we know them well, our conversation will be different according to circumstances: informal when you are taking part in the village football match ('Come on, Grindlethorpe, you can do it!'), but more careful and serious when someone has died ('I was very sorry to hear about William.'). Notice also that in both these circumstances we use set phrases and particular words.

Now notice another thing. When you are alone with one person you talk in an 'ordinary' way ('How much have we spent?'). But when you get up to speak at a public meeting, you may use words and ways of speaking which are peculiar and not part of your normal experience ('Can the treasurer give us the figures for current expenditure?'). All of this tells us something about prayer. Alone with God we will talk in a different way from when we are all worshipping together in church. In private prayer we may pray freely or in set forms. But it is particularly when we are all together in public worship that, as in a public meeting, we are put more 'on the spot' and will depend on things being run with some formality. It will be different in varying circumstances, but there will always be set forms and phrases. Whether we say to somebody 'Good morning', 'How do you do', or 'Hiya!', it has all been said many times before, and will be again. Whether our words are 'Come on, come on, you can do it!' or 'May I ask the chairman to make sure a greater effort is made?' the meaning is the same, but the circumstances are different. In both cases the words are entirely to be expected.

So it is that as Christians we find ourselves using set forms and stock phrases when we have things to say to God. And because God is not exactly like us, but in some ways very different, we find ourselves using some words which don't at first come naturally. This is one way in which relating to God is like relating to other people, but is at the same time different and unique.

A good example of this is the problem some people have with saying words of praise to God, for example:

> Blessed are you, Sovereign Lord,
> Almighty God and Father:
> to you be all glory and honour
> for ever and ever.

Surely the God of love does not need such high-flown praises? He doesn't want us to flatter him with all this pompous stuff. Our problem, however, comes from once again expecting the wrong thing. This is a good example of the way prayer does not quite correspond with ordinary life.

When we pray we know two things about God. One is that he is very near to us, and is our friend, our brother, sister, father and mother. He is very close to us indeed.

However, we also know that he is so different that words fail us. All we can do is use poetry – that is, words which don't just mean what they say, but which try to point beyond.

'Glory to you, our mighty Prime Minister' would sound bombastic and far from the humility which expresses true service. But 'Glory to you, Eternal Father, Almighty God' doesn't mean what it says: it is poetry which attempts to say the unsayable. It is not the language of bombast, but the language of love, where nothing can say too much about the one who is loved. To speak such words as these is not to grovel or flatter – it is a special language, the language of thanksgiving, praise and love. It is saying a poem to someone who deserves poems. If we simply take the words at face value we have missed the point. Poetry plays a very important role in our conversation with God. You only need think of the hundreds of hymns which people enjoy singing in church to realize that.

So far, we have hardly begun to say anything about prayer, and yet we have already found two ways in which we can learn about it from daily life. First of all, daily life is full of rituals and patterns, handshakes, waves, winks, set phrases, certain ways of doing things. Unless we are going to try to be something we aren't, then God is probably going to involve the same sort of thing too.

Second, we are wrong in thinking that prayer should always be intense, concentrated, or full of a seriousness which we try to turn on. We aren't made like that, and if we always try to pray in that way we shall either become discouraged, or give up, or turn on some behaviour which is not real. There is a great deal to be learned from this, which can help us to discover that in the business of praying we may have been making unnecessary difficulties for ourselves, and as a result we find it difficult to find God's presence in the newsagent's and all the other ordinary things of life.

We need to unlearn some habits and assumptions, if our prayer is to come naturally.

3 *Friends and strangers*

Life is full of surprises. When we are queueing for our *Radio Times* at the newsagent's most of the people in the queue are just faces. We do our best to weigh them up, but we can't discover much just from their appearance, and often we get them completely wrong.

Imagine you have bought a new house and today you move in. You can't find where anything is. You try to get one room straight and liveable-in. The time comes to prepare the evening meal – where's the potato peeler?

Can't find it anywhere. Looking out through the window you get a shock. The next-door neighbour is coming home. It's the man you see at the newsagent's in town. He always looks miserable, and probably bad-tempered. You have sometimes thought to yourself, 'I wonder if he's got many friends – I can't say I'd like to be one of them.' You don't fancy going round to borrow a potato-peeler, and you persuade young Andy to go to the chip-shop instead. However, Andy has a mind of his own, and goes to the man's house anyway.

He comes back with the man in tow, together with a potato-peeler. Your neighbour surprisingly turns out to be a comical Liverpudlian. They all want to welcome you with a drink – will you come round? Gary and Stella's house is a menagerie of children, cats, dogs and budgies. Stella works at the hairdresser's, and has done your hair plenty of times. Who would have guessed that these two passing faces in your life were married? You couldn't want more warm-hearted neighbours.

As time goes on, however, you discover more. They are marvellous neighbours, and you become the best of friends. But there's never a silver lining that hasn't a cloud behind it, and now you discover their drawbacks. For instance, they are noisy late at night. One source of irritation is their ancient dustbin with its metal lid, which stays on so well on this windy hilltop. The only problem is getting it on in the first place. They always use it just as you are dropping off to sleep. One night you rush down in your dressing-gown, and catch Gary in the act. He gets such an earful that he leaves the lid on the ground, rather than make more noise. A few minutes later, Stella, oblivious to this, comes down with some rubbish from Roxanne's room, kicks the lid in the dark and goes all her length, making more noise than ever. You rush down again, hopping mad, and shout 'You did that on purpose!', while a mystified Stella is still groping around on the ground in the dark.

In ways like this Gary and Stella and family are both a pleasure and a trial to you (and you are to them, if the truth were known).

Years later, after you have seen your children and theirs grow up together, and there has even been a marriage between two of them, so that you are now relations, you think back occasionally to the old days when those two were just faces in the newsagent's and the hairdresser's. People are full of surprises, you might probably think. How little we realize what lies behind appearances!

It takes time to get to know somebody. You may meet a very interesting person who is charm itself, well-dressed, likeable and amusing, and then discover that while you were in the kitchen making a cup of tea he has gone off with the milk money and the video. You thought you knew what he was like, and you didn't. If you belong to a community, whether it is a family, a firm, or a village, you will know how long it takes to get to know people, their strengths, their weaknesses, their preferences, habits and foibles. We never get to know it all, and first impressions nearly always deceive. This is one of the great and not so easy lessons that most newly-weds have to learn, that other people 'tick' in a very different way from you.

All of these things have something to tell us about knowing God. When it comes to knowing him, many Christians are stuck at the newsagent's or hairdresser's, where God is just a face. If that is so, we are still at the stage of first impressions.

15

We often picture God as very strange and unapproachable. We may find him impossible to talk to. Or we find him distant and half-hidden, somebody we are very uncertain of. It is all first impressions, because we have not yet come to know him very well. A tell-tale sign of this is having a desire for some inner experience when we pray and worship. We want to feel strengthened, reassured; to feel we are not just wasting our time. We want it all, all at once. We want a pay-off for all our effort in praying and in dragging ourselves to church.

We put the church itself under the same judgement. If a service doesn't suit us we stop going.

Daily life, as usual, is very helpful here in putting this in proportion. Any engaged couple who expect sudden bliss and perfect love are going to be disillusioned before very long. Not only is the other person often disappointing me, but I am disappointing them. The other person is a mystery. We all know what the recipe is – or we soon will: getting to know somebody is a hard slog. It has to be worked at, and it won't be full of beautiful feelings all the time. If husband and wife are to grow together and survive in marriage, they need a small dash of soul and poetry, but a mountain of nitty-gritty. There is no reason why we should expect things to be any different in our relationship with God.

When we pray, we may need to keep reminding ourselves at the start that the poetry and the soulfulness in it will need to be accompanied by a mountain of nitty-gritty. Getting to know God is like getting to know any other people: it can demand from us a good deal of care, patience and perseverance.

God is our friend even before we ask; he has given himself totally to us. But we are very different from him, and there is no way around that. There are no short cuts. Our ways are not his ways, and our thoughts are not his thoughts (Isaiah 55.8). Getting to know him will involve a long journey. We should never be satisfied with the mere face we see on first acquaintance, yet that is all we have when we start. Our picture of God is a first impression, wide of the mark.

Having said all that, we now need to look at the other side. For there are times when we are consoled and strengthened, and we think we have come a little nearer to God. There are times in prayer and in worship when we feel we have received something, when we get a sense of God's presence. And yet, what happens? It fades. We are great forgetters. We can have a moving experience in church and a couple of hours later be back at our gossip and backbiting, our complaints and deceptions. We are like kettles. In the old days they used to be kept on the side of the hob. They quietly tinkled away, standing over the glowing coals, always ready for use whenever we wanted to make a cup of tea. Now the old fireplace has gone – we have to turn on the electric kettle each time we need it, and it goes cold again very quickly. Sunday worship brings us back to the boil. But we quickly go cold, and we need to be brought back to the boil again and again. That is why we have to pray regularly. We quickly forget, and if we continue to do that, God will always remain someone we know only very slightly. Then we are bound to misunderstand him.

Christian worship has always laid great emphasis on remembering and reminding. Our worship in church tells the story over and over again. 'Remember,' it says, and each time we pray, we are remembering, paying a

call on God much as if he were our next-door neighbour, and so getting to know him a little better. We
quickly go cold – we forget. Prayer and worship remind
us once again, they bring us back to the boil, they warm
our faith that is always threatening to go cold.

We don't know God well, and in order to get to know
him better than we do, we need to work at it. Not only
that, but we need to persevere – and this is the job of a
lifetime, full of rewards if we are prepared to give ourselves to him as he gives himself to us.

4 *How can I believe that?*

When you used to see the stranger each day in the news-agent's, you knew nothing about him. It was only later, after getting to know Gary and his family, that you began to have an opinion about them. Yet we try to do the opposite with God – to say what we think of him before we know him. We think we have to believe this and that about God before we can start worshipping, and that means coming to an opinion about him from the start. There is something in this, but on its own it is not the whole truth. Because of this strange way in which we go about things, many people don't bother with Christianity: they have too much difficulty in believing. They say, 'I can't believe those things, so how can I start?' That's the wrong way around, just as it is with Gary and Stella. We have to trust first. Growth in knowledge about them follows on from our trust.

Even those of us who go to church can find this a stumbling-block. There are people who don't join in saying certain phrases in the Creed on Sunday because there are parts they can't believe. When we do that we are expecting the wrong thing of the Creed. Why put so much emphasis on what we believe? People who get married are in the dark about what it is going to mean. Within the family we are always in some ways a mystery to each other. While husband and wife can often sense what the other is thinking or feeling, the other person always remains 'other', a mystery. With children this progresses as it goes along – parents are never sure which way their children's behaviour will turn next. A classic case of this lack of comprehension is found in marriage breakdown. The crisis can come as a surprise to both partners, but usually more to one than to the other. This person used to love me, but now claims not to – we are filled with a disbelief which refuses to go away. We are incapable of believing it. We may make great efforts to accept that our partner's love for us has died, but the disbelief is so strong that it won't let us accept.

If the behaviour of husbands or daughters can be beyond belief, then sometimes God's own behaviour will take some believing too. If knowing people depended on believing things about them, then we would never get to know anybody.

We have the wrong end of the stick. Of course, believing things is important, but it doesn't have to be the place where we start. If being a Christian is only about believing certain things, that is not much better than jumping through hoops. To believe that some things are true is, on its own, nothing better than doing performing tricks with our brains. We can find plenty of religions, sects and movements which are like this. Their followers have to leave their common sense on one side. Many religions, and many versions of Christianity, are like the song about Parliament in Gilbert and Sullivan's *Iolanthe*: 'When in that House MPs divide . . . they've got to leave [their] brains outside.' In this type of religion we are asked to swallow something so far-fetched that we have to turn off our common sense while we do it. Unfortunately there is plenty of such religion around. It is hardly surprising that people often can't take Christianity seriously. They are put off by these things, and come to the conclusion that all religion must be the same.

Mainstream Christianity has always taken common sense seriously. It does not ask us to turn our brains off, nor does it seek to escape from what is real. It doesn't look for a dream world; it looks at real daily life. Christianity is not a business of believing this and that about many things: it centres on something quite different – belief in a person. Not belief-about, but belief-in.

There is great confusion here, because the word 'belief' means two things. One is, believing some things to be true, like 'I believe that the earth goes around the sun.' The other meaning is belief-in, to believe in a person or an ideal. 'I believe in being honest', for instance. For Christians, believing that certain facts about God are true is impossible without the other sort of belief: belief-in.

Another word for belief-in is 'trust'. Trust should never be confused with holding particular beliefs. Being Christians has to do with knowing a person, in just the same way as friendship is about knowing (and trusting) a person. This is made clear if we ask: What is the most important thing about our parents – that we know about them, or that we know them? It must be the second. It is more important that I know my mother than that I just know some things about her. So it is more important to know God than simply to know certain things about him. We have to start not so much with belief, but with doing.

Christianity, surprisingly, starts most often with the question, 'What must I do?', rather than with asking, 'What must I believe?' At this point let us meet one of many people in the New Testament who asked the question, 'What must I do?' – it is the jailer who let Paul out of prison. The answer was: 'Believe in Jesus Christ and so be saved' (Acts 16.31). Paul was talking of belief-in. Belief in a person is totally different from mere belief about them. It is concerned not merely with information, but with a relationship. The Creed starts, 'I believe in . . .'. It does not start, 'I believe that . . .'. In other words, it does not ask us for an opinion about ideas. It is an invitation to trust a person.

Most people in fact, if they really thought about it, are not asking first of all what things they are supposed to believe. They are asking another question: 'Who can I trust?' And very often there is a further question to accompany it: 'What must I do?' This question crops up many times in the New Testament. Not, 'What must I believe?' but 'What must I do?' This is the question the rich young man asked of Jesus (Matthew 19.16–22). Jesus saw what he was capable of, and replied, 'Give everything away and follow me.' Then there was the crowd in Jerusalem which listened to Peter's speech at Pentecost. It was not about beliefs that they asked, but 'What shall we do?' (Acts 2.37)

When we say the Creed in church, then, are all these beliefs a waste of time? Don't we need to believe any of the Church's teachings? Yes, we do. They are at the heart of the Christian life. But it is not simply a matter of believing that some things happened, like the Resurrection, or the Virgin Birth (although it is indeed that as well). It is a matter of learning to take that story and make it our own. We are encouraged to make friends with that story because Christ has given us a taste of something we sense we can trust.

For example, when we say, 'He ascended into heaven', we may think, 'I can't believe that, so I can't say it.' If so, we have mistaken what it is about. We are not expected to swallow strange things on a spoon, as we might have been given cod-liver oil as children. We are invited to start up a conversation with the Church's inherited treasure-house. If we see doctrines not as pills but as friends, then something different starts to happen. Then we can say, 'Ascension of Jesus, I don't understand you, but I am prepared to start a conversation with you.' If we do that, we will begin to discover that we were approaching it in the wrong way before.

It is like being an apprentice gardener. At the start we may think that dandelions and bindweed are beautiful.

It takes us some time to learn that in a cultivated garden they are pests. Then our experience grows, and we begin to learn the wisdom of the garden. We learn about fertilizers, about pruning, about knowing what this soil is best for, and all that deep expertise which in a seasoned gardener is partly learned by experience and partly handed on from person to person, from book to book. There is a world of inherited wisdom to take on board. The more of it we learn, the more different the garden appears.

It is similar with the ascension of Jesus. We need to put on one side for now the fact that perhaps we may not be able to believe it happened as it is recounted in the story. Instead we need to enter into a conversation with the story, and come gradually to know it as a friend. In that way we can learn that it says many things, not only to the mind, but also to the feelings and to our 'bones'.

It is natural to say 'I can't believe that stuff, and therefore I can't be a Christian.' In fact, however, when we say that, we are coming at things the wrong way around. The beliefs of the Church are like photographs in a family album. What is most real is the family, not the album. If we want to know Gary and Stella we don't start with the photos. Some of them will be bad ones, and none of them will show us everything. They won't show us how the person laughs, talks, or walks. Nor their manner, their sense of humour, or their character. In fact, photos can be very misleading. However, for Gary and Stella themselves, and for their friends and next-door neighbours, looking at photos can be very entertaining. That is because the photos capture something about Gary and Stella.

It is like that with belief. Trying to believe all of the Creed (the photograph album of Christian life) only means something after long experience. Christian belief is a journey of discovery, which can only start if we are already trying to do it.

There is a difference from photograph albums, however. The main difference is that families don't need photographs. They were quite happy for thousands of years without them. The Church, on the other hand, needs to say something about what she believes because, as in any very large extended family, people can get out of touch and start going off, each on their own sweet way. The Church is so old (two thousand years) that memories become very dim, and we have to keep some sort of check on whether we are all continuing to go the same way together.

Creeds are therefore like identity cards and passports. Without passports and cards, it would be impossible to run libraries, cars, and package holidays. There are too many of us, all unknown to each other – the whole thing without such documents would be a mess.

But I don't join a library in order to have a library ticket. And I don't book a holiday to Ibiza in order to get a passport photograph. It's the other way around. The photo is just one of the things you need in order to get to Ibiza. It is similar with the Church's beliefs. They are one of the means of keeping us together with Christ. But we don't cancel a holiday to Ibiza if our passport photo is a bad one. And we don't stop going to Church or saying the Creed just because we aren't at ease with all of it.

The difficulty comes, however, when we move beyond seeing the beliefs just as photographs. There is a hitch here, and it is that in the end belief requires of us some sort of assent, some kind of acceptance. In other words, it does ask for a degree of faith, of putting our trust in some things we cannot fully see. Ultimately we have to say that belief is not something we can turn on – it can only come as a gift from God. In the end the doctrines of the Christian faith are more than mere photographs. They need to be embraced, like people. But we need not worry too much if it takes us some time to get there. And while we are struggling, all that is asked of us is that we look upon them with good will and openness.

We should not be put off by our first impressions of God or of the Church. Our first impressions of people are nearly always wide of the mark. We need to persevere, and God will be faithful to us, and will make himself known to us. Gradually, in this way, we shall come to discover that, without noticing it happening, we have moved house and become his next-door neighbour.

5 *Layers*

What is going on inside me? I'm not sure. We all understand quite a lot about ourselves, but we are far from knowing everything. None of us knows what is really going on inside.

Say, for example, you meet someone in the street and have a conversation with them. You come away from it feeling very uneasy, but can't put your finger on it. What is going on inside you to make you feel uneasy?

Or again, you have a night out at the cinema, and the film is so marvellous that you feel on top of the world.

Or you have a short holiday and come back feeling fantastic – ready for anything. What has gone on inside that makes everything different now? You were 'cheesed off' and drooping a week ago.

We are like an onion. Our inside has many layers to it, and we can't see them all. A good example of the way we are onion-like is learning to do some complicated task such as driving a car. At the start you have to think out every move.

'No, Mr Arkwright,' says the instructress wearily. 'You have to push down the clutch before you change gear.'

Mr Arkwright fumbles about with the wrong foot while trying to remember to keep control of the wheel.

'Don't forget the rear mirror,' she suddenly screams. After a few lessons, however, he does it without thinking.

We are like onions. We live in our top layer, forgetting that at other layers we are 'doing things without thinking'. Even when you are an experienced driver you can have horrible surprises. On a long journey you suddenly realize that for the last ten minutes you have been driving along a twisting road full of traffic, but can remember nothing about it. You have been 'miles away'. Another layer of your onion has been driving for you. Learning a foreign language is a similar experience. At the start it all flows over you like gobbledygook, however well you have studied the language. But gradually the mist clears, and by some strange inner working of the human mind, you find the language has come alive inside you, and you talk and listen with increasing confidence. You have done it without noticing it.

There is an infinite number of ways in which our hidden layers work. They can drastically affect our everyday life, such as when we become angry or irritable for no apparent reason – then the doctor tells us we are overtired, or suffering from stress, and we realize that something has been going on inside us unseen and un-noticed, something which has changed us.

Another way this works is in our friendships and our loves. Husbands and wives often sense things about their partner without anything being said. They also continue to love each other without expressing it much in words or actions. It simply lives down there, a large part of the time, in our unseen layers.

We forget all of this when we pray. We think that when we are praying we should 'feel' something at the top layer of our onion. The real pay-off, however, as in marriage, comes uninvited and unsought. It comes from being faithful and persevering, day in and day out. It comes at other layers, not just the top one. When we pray, we should always remember this – it is the first thing to remember about being a Christian – leave it to your layers. Some people pray as if there is a need to squeeze every drop of experience out of every second. So they are anxious about their prayer, and anxious about God without realizing it. We ought to relax, just get on with our prayers, and leave all the rest to our onion-layers. If God wants to declare something to you in the top layer of your mind, he will do so. We are not to worry. God's workings are largely hidden.

What is true of prayer is true also of listening to read-ings from the Bible. So many words! Our services seem to have far too many. Once again, we have to think of it in the long term. We can't concentrate on all the read-ings. In fact, that is not the only way of listening to them. One of the most important ways of listening to the Bible is to let it all flow over us. We might not realize it, but over the years we are gradually becoming steeped in it. When we listen to the Bible being read, a lot of it may go over our heads. But every now and then there are nuggets. There are bits that we get something out of.

We need to listen to the scriptures as if we are waiting for nuggets. Like a fielder in a game of cricket, every now and then a ball comes our way. It may be a particular story, or it could be just a sentence which catches our attention. Part of the reason why we have Bible readings in church is that it is worth it for the nuggets – even if there are some occasions when we find no nuggets in it.

But this is not the only reason. Here we go back to what we have said about remembering. When we hear the scriptures being read aloud in church, we are going over 'the greatest story ever told'. From Adam and Eve to Moses. From Moses to the prophets. From the prophets to Jesus, and then on to Paul and the story of the apostles. It is a long, long serial story. Like *Coronation Street* or *Neighbours*, the story goes on and on, returning again and again to the same situations.

One reason why we read the Bible in church is so that we shall come to have the whole story in our bones, or rather, in our onion-layers. If that is to come about, then we shall read the tedious parts as well as the interesting ones, the difficult as well as the easy. Children look forward to hearing the same story over and over again, and they correct you if you leave a bit out. They are right – the story has to be respected, and we cannot miss out certain parts simply because we think they are tedious. We need to see every reading as part of one of the longest videos ever shown. All of it belongs together.

In fact, once we think about it, all of our worship is soaked in scripture. The Bible is our daily bread. It appears in the prayers, in the hymns, the canticles and psalms and even the stained-glass windows. We are living in it, swimming in God's Word, breathing it in, the Word of Life. Every service in church is scattered with God's nuggets. They are there not only to teach us but also to kindle us, to set us aflame. They help us turn the whole of our person to him. We should let scripture flow over us – let it pickle us in salvation-history.

It is the same both for the scriptures and for our prayers. We don't need to keep 'feeling' something all the time. It isn't part of our nature to be like that. We can't see all our onion-layers. When we pray, and when we listen to the scriptures, our layers are being touched and changed in ways that we can't see.

In our prayers, therefore, we have to be like the man in the parable who planted his seed and then left it to get on with growing (Mark 4.26–9). He didn't keep worrying about whether it was all right. We need simply to get on with doing the job, and leave it to God and our onion-layers to produce the results. Otherwise we shall be like a person who puts a new plant in the garden and then keeps digging it up to see how the roots are doing.

We can't help judging our prayer and trying to tell whether it is going all right. We look for results, and that is only sensible and right. However, when we do this we only tend to look at the top layer – we ignore the other hidden parts of our onion. God prefers the hidden ways to the limelight. He works in ways that we cannot see, with results that we would not expect. In other words, we need to carry on in faith – just have faith in the sheer doing of it. Leave the rest to God.

6 *In the family*

The Church often disappoints us. But we are discovering, I hope, that this is often because we have been going at things in the wrong way. Christians have developed bad habits. Then they can't understand why they fail to be satisfied. It is time now to look at a particularly bad habit which lies close to the heart of our problems. Put simply, it is that we think too much in terms of 'me', and not enough in terms of 'we'.

Imagine a football team. After winning a famous match the whole team is interviewed on television. The manager says, 'I am very pleased with the way my strategy worked.' The captain says, 'I was a bit worried at times, but everything started to go my way in the second half.' The right winger says, 'I wasn't very happy with my performance until I scored the first goal.' There is something wrong with this football team. In fact it can't exist, because no team which talked always about 'I' and 'me' could ever win a match. Footballers in real life find themselves talking about 'us' a lot of the time. They think as a team.

Another example is a family. A mother who always talks about herself and never about the children is a strange mother. A husband who thinks all the time about number one will be a disaster as a husband and father. Members of families in fact sometimes use 'I' and sometimes use 'we', depending on the circumstances.

When we think to ourselves about God, we tend to use 'I' most of the time. We talk about 'my faith', 'my prayers', 'I believe'. We say, 'I can't get anywhere with prayer.' We would never think of saying, 'We can't get anywhere with prayer.' And yet look at the Lord's Prayer: Jesus didn't teach us to say, 'My Father . . . give me this day my daily bread'. We are to use 'our' and 'us'. 'Our Father'.

When we pray, we can feel very alone. Our prayer may seem a poor effort. Some of the words seem unreal, and we feel inadequate. There I am, alone under God's spotlight, and if he is there he must think this is a weak effort as he looks down on me. And I am thinking to myself, 'How am I doing? Not very well.' And whether I pray by myself, or with other people in church, it feels like a lonely 'me' trying to get through to a God who is also alone.

Why have we ended up thinking in this way? It goes back a long way, over many hundreds of years, something our grandparents have passed on to us. But when we look at the great teachers of Christian prayer, the saints of past ages, and when we look at Jesus himself, we find that we have been wrong. It is 'Our Father' before it is 'My Father', it is our prayer before it is my prayer. There is a sense in which there is no such thing as 'private' prayer for Christians. When we were baptized we became members of a family, the Church. It is like the football team described above. We have to learn to say 'us' as well as 'me'. So Saint Cyprian, who lived in the third century, could say, 'Our prayer is . . . shared; and when we pray, we pray not for one, but for the whole people, because we the whole people are one.' In the New Testament itself, St Paul tells us that we are one body, not isolated individuals. We all make up one body. 'The eye cannot say to the hand, "I do not need you,"; or the head to the feet, "I do not need you" ' (1 Corinthians 12.21 NEB). So then, when I pray, I am not alone. I have been baptized, and I am a member of the body. I have to pray like a football team plays football – never as 'me' alone, even when there is not another soul around, even when I am in great desolation. A member of the Orthodox Church puts it in this way: 'Nobody is a Christian by himself, but only as a member of the Body. Even in solitude, "in the chamber", a Christian prays as a member of the redeemed community, the Church.'[1]

Because of this the place where our prayer needs to start is in our baptism and in the eucharist or communion. Through the waters of baptism we become members of Christ's Body. The tone is then set for all our prayer. It is something we do together. Therefore its centre and heart is the holy table, the bread and the wine which we share. It starts here because communion is about community.

Does this mean that Christians shouldn't pray on their own? Far from it. Prayer on our own is important and necessary. But when we know we are not alone, it is transformed: for we now realize it is all part of a team effort, and that we all belong together. No wonder that we can't find God – we are trying to do it all in private, and he will never be found that way.

What, then, must we do? The whole of this book is an attempt to answer that question, but there is one aspect of it which is the particular concern of this chapter. It is the business of discovering that we are not alone, and we can't be alone. When we are seeking God out, we ought to remember that many other people are doing so at the same time. When we pray, millions of people all over the world are praying with us. There may be someone next door or around the corner who, unknown to us, is praying. There will certainly be people in many countries praying at the same time as you. The Lord's Prayer is said so often, by so many people, that we know at the time we are saying it, that there will be Italians, Americans, Russians, Eskimos, and people from very different worlds, whom we will never meet, saying it in time with us.

More remarkable still, they also will be thinking of us. In the words of Petru Dumitriu,

> Let us think of those who think of us without knowing us, let us think of those who pray, of all the silent multitude of souls at prayer. We are not alone. In solitude, silence, forgiveness, in the sleep of matter, the sound and fury of suffering, of birth, of coupling, of despair, of evil and of good, there is everywhere the peace of prayer, everywhere glimmers of grace; there is the Church of souls.[2]

All of creation is reaching out to God – a great song in which we are all invited to sing. In the book of Revelation we read:

> I heard every created thing in heaven and on earth,
> and under the earth and in the sea,
> all that is in them, crying out.
>
> (Revelation 5.13 NEB)

Once we know that this is the case, everything is changed, our chains begin to fall away. Prayer is now like singing 'Auld Lang Syne' on New Year's Eve. If we were asked at a party to get up and sing Auld Lang Syne on our own, we might well be terrified. Because of our nerves we might make an even worse performance than it need have been. But when we are singing together with everybody, we are all caught up together, and there will be no nerves, no doubts about our voice. We can bawl it as badly as we like, because we are not alone. Prayer comes most naturally when we have a sense of doing it together.

This leads on to another thing. When we pray, not only do we mistakenly think of ourselves as being alone.

We also think of God as being alone. In fact he is not. Because of the mysterious business of the Trinity, it is impossible to pin God down with a simple picture inside our head. God is one God. But he is also three: the Father, the Son, and the Holy Spirit. If we watch championship ballroom dancing, we might sometimes think, 'Is it two people, or is it one?' – they move so perfectly together. With God, we can feel the same: Is it three, or is it one? Sometimes we pray to Christ, sometimes to the Holy Spirit, sometimes to God the Father. (We waltz with one or the other.) Sometimes we pray to all three (doing the Gay Gordons), sometimes we pass from hand to hand (then it is a square dance). So one of the oldest wordings of the Gloria runs:

> Glory to the Father,
> through the Son,
> In the Holy Spirit.

To our brain all of this is double-dutch. However, as we know from science magazines, fact is often stranger than fiction. Our insights into molecules and atoms, and into the inner workings of the universe, have shown us things that are utterly mind-boggling – that travelling through space makes time go more slowly, or that the universe is curved; that what we thought were the laws of nature apply only in our little world, but begin to do very peculiar things the more closely we look into them. It is therefore not entirely surprising that God, the mystery at the heart of the universe, should be impossible to describe. Nor should it be a complete surprise that we should find ourselves having to talk in terms of him being both three and one. The three persons dance together, never alone. Are they three or are they one? Is it they? Or he? Or she? And the Trinity is wanting to take us up into the dance.

Sometimes we may think, 'Which partner am I with at the moment? Am I praying to Jesus, or to the Father? Or am I praying to·the Spirit?' The important thing about dancing is to give ourself up to it, without thinking where we are putting our feet. We can ask all kinds of awkward questions about the Trinity. We should carry on asking them – that is the whole point. It is a teaser because God is a teaser. But we should carry on meeting him too, and making his acquaintance in the dance of prayer.

There is still more to it. There are, gathered to God, all the saints and the souls of those who have died. 'After that I looked and saw a vast throng, which no one could number, from all races and tribes, nations and languages, standing before the throne . . .' (Revelation 7.9 REB). The patriarchs and prophets, the apostles and evangelists, the martyrs and all who have witnessed to the truth, to love, to peace and to justice – a great family, together with Mary the mother of the Lord, and all who were close to him during his time on earth and in all the centuries that have followed, right up to this very day. And together with them, we are not quite sure how, there are all those who have died, the good and the bad, the lovely and the unlovely. Somehow they are continuing their pilgrimage, united with us, we hope and pray, because they as well are praying and seeking, until the final day, when the secrets of all hearts will be revealed.

Therefore, even if a nuclear bomb should destroy the earth, and you were the last person left in existence, you still would not be alone in prayer. You would still know Christ and the company of the saints.

There is still one more thing we need to realize, and this is somewhat more difficult than the others. So far we have described a great crowd on earth, and then, across the divide, a great crowd 'beyond the veil'. Seen simply like that, it might seem like two separate football teams. But that can't be so. The Church is one lot, not two lots of people. Here is the most suprising thing. The two worlds are all mingled together. This finally blows apart our mistaken ideas about God and prayer.

It could be put in this way: if it is all one great dance, who is doing the dancing? We are – all caught up in it together. When I pray, who is praying? Well, I am praying by myself. On the other hand, Jesus is praying in me. So is the Holy Spirit (Romans 8.26). If we go back to pickled onions, it is like trying to answer the question: 'Is it all onion, or is it all vinegar?' The onion and the vinegar within it are all one thing. And Christ is in me and I in him. The saints are singing their eternal song, and they are singing it in me. But they take up my words too, and sing them in heaven, so I am praying in them. Above all, it is the endless, love-filled prayer of the Holy Trinity which sweeps us up into its movement, so we no longer know quite what is going on.

St Paul tried various ways of putting it: in one place he says, 'I live no longer, but Christ lives in me' (Galatians 2.20). In Romans (8.15) he says, 'When we cry, Abba! Father! it is the Spirit himself bearing witness with our spirit'. And then in the famous passage in Galatians (4.6) he tells us, 'God has sent the Spirit of his Son into our hearts, crying, Abba! Father!' The Prayer of Humble Access in the Anglican liturgy prays that 'he may dwell in us, and we in him'. This reminds us of John 17.21: 'Father, may they be one in us, as you are in me and I in you.' All of this is trying to put into words something that is beyond words. It is trying to say that when we pray we are praying with all the Church, but not in an us-and-them kind of way. It is all pickled up together, one people and one song. My prayer is not just my prayer. It 'booms' or echoes, as our voices do in a bathroom or a cathedral; it is magnified, glorified, made magnificent. It is the song of the universe. It is because of all of this that in the great thanksgiving prayer of the eucharist, we say at one point, '. . . with angels and archangels and all the company of heaven', and then by the time we get to the end of the prayer we have moved on from the saints to the divine dance itself:

> By whom, and with whom, and in whom,
> in the unity of the Holy Spirit,
> all honour and glory be yours,
> Almighty Father, now and for ever. Amen.[3]

So we can't just talk about 'my' prayers. We can't just say 'I praise you', or, 'I ask this'. That doesn't mean that I stop being 'me'. It doesn't mean that I get swallowed up in some anonymous crowd. It means the complete opposite. It sets me free to become myself. In places where there is a strong community life (such as a village) you can often find some real characters. The individual and the community – the one needs the other. We run into trouble if either of them gets out of hand. Communism was one result of that. Our modern selfishness and individualism are the other.

In this chapter we have been trying to set the balance straight. We are people who are repeating, like a gramophone record which has got stuck in a groove, 'I, I, I'. If we learn also to repeat, 'we, we, we', then something bigger and better than both grows out of it. Then, when we pray as 'we' together in church, there will be a background tune of 'I, I, I'.

Conversely, when I pray alone, there will be another music always in the background: 'we, we, we'.

1 Kallistos Ware, *The Orthodox Church* (Penguin 1969), p. 310.
2 P. Dumitriu, *To the Unknown God* (Collins 1982), pp. 152f.
3 *The Alternative Service Book 1980*, The Order for Holy Communion, Rite A, Third Eucharistic Prayer, p. 141. Copyright © The Central Board of Finance of the Church of England 1980.

7 *Something special*

It is very interesting to think how we would relate to each other if we were invisible and untouchable, like gas or ghosts. Can you offer someone who is all gas a cup of tea? Can you shake hands with a ghost, or would your hand go straight through them?

Or again, notice how difficult it is to talk to people on the telephone. It's much better to see them face to face. Somehow we can't explain everything properly over the phone. Something necessary is missing. In knowing people and getting on with them day by day we need if possible to see them, hear them and touch them. We need to see their faces, shake their hands, touch them on the arm, make them laugh. On special occasions we need to give them things, flowers or chocolates, or send a card. Often we need to do something special such as hold a party, or go to the pictures. When you think of it, our daily come-and-go with people is very physical.

When it comes to God, we change the rules completely. We seem to think that it can be all gas and ghosts. You might reply, 'St John says God is a spirit' (John 4.24). But the scriptures say he is many other things too: fire, flesh, rock, bread and wine, water, Christ Jesus (a human being), the Body of Christ, love (whoever heard of love without flesh and blood?), fortress, angel, lamb, door, and much more.

We seem to think prayer is a kind of faceless telephone-call. Why should we think God would be satisfied with the telephone? It can indeed be like that, of course. And the telephone can be adequate for its purpose. There are plenty who have phoned up their beloved every day and depended on it. But if that is all they will ever get, it's not good enough by half. If we are going to have any chance of getting to know God, then we need to see him, to hear, to touch him. We need to look into his face and watch his gestures, to hear his words and know that he hears and sees and touches us in return. What are we asking of people if we tell them to pray as if God were a ghost, a dumb, invisible man?

Now here we have a tall order. Surely, God is invisible. 'No one has ever seen God', says St John (John 1.18). We are beginning to learn, however, that the Bible says things by opposites. God is both like us and he isn't. Everything we say about him is partly true, partly not. So when we ask, 'Is it possible to see God?',

43

the Bible replies, 'It is and it isn't.' We can't hope to see God. But St John's gospel gives us the other side of the picture, when Jesus says, 'Whoever has seen me has seen the Father' (John 14.9). There is no doubt that for the disciples and the early followers of Jesus there was a feeling that here they were meeting God. As time passed they came more and more to realize this. You will say, 'That's all very good. But Jesus came and Jesus went. Now what do we do? Where can we see God now?'

What in fact happened can be put in this way. The Spirit came on the disciples at Pentecost. While, before all this, people had seen God in Jesus, now they saw him in the disciples. They had become in their turn the Body of Christ. The physical presence of Jesus now continues in his Church, spread out among all his people. The Church is a physical body. It is seeable, hearable, touchable. It has its particular habits, its gestures, its ways of doing things. It has its own ways of 'saying something special'. In a way the bread and the wine at the eucharist are like a bunch of flowers or a box of chocolates when we use those things to say something special. In another way the church building has that purpose, which is why we lavish so much care on it, the pictures, the decorations, the flowers, the paint, and the polish.

This is just how we behave in everyday life too, except that some of it is in a different style. In ordinary life we wave, embrace, kiss, shake hands, we dance, we stand up for some things, sit down for others. We wear different clothes for different occasions, we make a ritual of evenings out, or entertaining guests. In all of these ways we give expression to the business of being with other people. And so we do similar things to express our being with God. In fact, as Christians, the first thing we are looking for is something to do. When St Paul, was knocked from his horse on the road to Damascus, the first words that sprang to his lips were: 'What must I do, Lord?' (Acts 22.9).

Notice three things about our need to do something. The first is that we need a church building in just the same way as we need a home for ourselves. It is important to us (usually) to try to keep our home nice. It is important to us to wear clothes of a certain kind, to have a bit of music about the place, a few flowers, knick-knacks, keepsakes and heirlooms. That is very natural. It is true also of the church building. The church with all its paraphernalia is a way of being at home with God.

Second, we need patterned ways of doing things. In our ordinary daily life we need elements of ritual, pattern and habit, which help to make the world go round. We need them in ordinary life, and we need them with God. All of these things meet our need to see and hear and touch him. In the church there is plenty to see, to touch, and to share. In this place we receive some answer to our desire to see and touch God. And that happens not because of bricks and stone. The place is only holy because of the people who meet in it and to whom it belongs. It is holy because of what we do there.

This leads on to one of the great lessons which Jesus had to bring to humanity. We see God in each other. It is hard to believe that when I am standing in the newsagent's, God is in the customers. It becomes believable, on the other hand, when I am in church. There it is possible to begin to see God in the other people worshipping with us, and co-operating together in offering the worship. From the church we learn the knack. Then we have to go out and sharpen it up in the newsagent's.

Although we are all sinners, bad advertisements for Christianity, enough to put anybody off, yet to live the gospel is to discover that in another person's face we are glimpsing the face of God.

If that is so, then we are to treat them in the knowledge that God is in them. Here we meet yet another person in the New Testament who asked, 'What must I do?' It is the teacher of the law in St Luke's gospel. 'Love God,' said Jesus, 'and love your neighbour' (Luke 10.25–37). As Jesus said of the poor and the hungry: 'Whatever you do to these, you have done to me' (Matthew 25.40). That is a very difficult thing to believe sometimes, but if we take all these things together and live them out, we find that it comes true.

The only kind of people we can relate to easily are living flesh and blood. God has given us that in the Church. To say that God is an invisible spirit is part of the truth, but not all the truth. The coming of Jesus meant that from now on God would be also touchable, smellable, hearable and seeable.

There it is, God's family, living flesh and blood. And just as our daily life is full of sight, sound, and smell, of touches, nods, and smiles, so the worship of the Church is something physical. In some ways it is the same as daily life – for example both in church and at home, we put flowers in vases, pictures on the wall, and we talk and we sing.

But it is also different from ordinary life, foreign to it – so the clergy wear robes, and we use special furniture, music, silence, incense, candles. God is at the same time both very everyday, and also very different. Although we need church buildings, God can be worshipped anywhere, and isn't tied to any buildings or places. This means that the whole experience can be taken home. That is the next thing we need to look at: using the Church as a take-away, bringing its worship home to assist us in praying.

8 *Take-away prayer*

We are happy to pray in church, but aren't so comfortable with praying together in the home. One of the answers to this problem is to take home some of the things we do in church. Just as we have found that in daily life and in church we tend to use all kinds of physical ways of expressing ourselves, at home too these are likely to be of great help to us.

To begin with, it is good to have a cross or a picture to use for our prayers. One form of Christian picture which is coming to be used by more and more people is the icon. You can't describe an icon, it needs to be seen.

There are icons of Christ, of the saints, of episodes from the Bible. In the homes of eastern Christians there is always an icon corner, where many icons are hung together on the wall, forming a focus for prayer. As well as being a focus, they are a presence. They say to us every time we look at them, 'Christ is here.' We don't even need to look at them. They may be behind us as we are watching the news on television. But it is enough to know they are there. Something like this is necessary for every Christian home. I know a family who have a 'prayer-shelf', with icons and other bits and pieces from holy places visited, and with cuttings from the newspaper, and pieces of paper with names of people who need to be prayed for, and prayers, hymns, and psalms scattered on it. It is a very ancient practice to light a candle (or, more safely, a night-light) when we pray. The living flame has that life about it that we also find in sitting by an open fire. Hindus ring a bell when they pray, and bring flowers. We usually only ring bells in towers nowadays, but in some parts of the world there are still Christians who use small bells, cymbals, triangles and even castanets. They are all there in the scriptures – see for instance Psalm 150.

As well as using pictures and candles, we need to use other ways of praying which involve our bodies. It is a profound need for us that sometimes our prayer should be physical: that we arrange some flowers, or light a candle; that we kneel (perhaps with the aid of a prayer-stool – these are easily made, and a picture is given at the end of this book), or that we make the sign of the cross, touching first our head, then our breast, then the left and the right shoulders, acting out as in a parable our calling to be people of the cross and the resurrection of Christ.

Or we might extend our hands, or perhaps sway like the Jews do when they pray. There are many ways of praying with our bodies, and many reasons why it is important. Some of them have already been given above. It is natural. We expect to relate physically to other people, so how can we hope to manage with God without physical expression?

As we have seen, our minds wander so much that we depend on our body to do some praying. We can't concentrate all the time. It is unnatural. While our mind comes and goes, the physical side needs to be there to hold it all together. And if you can't believe you are really praying when your mind wanders, it is good to remember that the onion still gets pickled even without thinking about it. Prayer is God's work, not just ours. His grace works like an infra-red lamp, or like the x-ray. Sometimes we can't feel anything. We can't see anything. But God's sovereign grace works on us just the same, just by our sitting in it.

Another outstanding reason why physical prayer is important is because it is easier to DO something together in the family, than it is to SAY something. Most families are too embarrassed to say prayers together. If there is something to do, that makes things easier. To light a candle in the icon corner and leave it burning for a while is a good start. When you are used to that, you could try simply reciting a prayer together (such as the Lord's Prayer) as it is lit. Then just get on with what you are doing while the candle burns, and blow it out after a certain time. In this way a small space of time has been marked out as God's. It is a start.

Another form of prayer which has always been a favourite is saying the poetry of the Bible, and especially the Psalms. The Psalms are the bread and butter of Christian prayer. We need the Psalms – they are a sheer gift to every person who seeks to pray. To start with, we all have our favourites, such as Psalm 23:

> The Lord is my shepherd, I shall not be in want.
> He makes me lie down in green pastures
>   and leads me beside still waters.
> He revives my soul
>   and guides me along right pathways for his
>   name's sake . . .

or Psalm 84:

How dear to me is your dwelling, O Lord of hosts;
My soul has a desire and longing for the courts of the Lord;
My heart and my flesh rejoice in the living God.
The sparrow has found her a house
    and the swallow a nest where she may lay her young;
by the side of your altars, O Lord of hosts,
    my King and my God.
Happy are the people whose strength is in you,
whose hearts are set on the pilgrims' way.
Those who go through the desolate valley
    will find it a place of springs,
for the early rains have covered it
    with pools of water . . .[1]

There are psalms for every kind of occasion, and all manner of need. At first they may seem strange or not very meaningful, but we have to get to know them as friends. As we say or sing the Psalms day by day, the veil is drawn back, the mist begins to clear, and we come to know that we belong, we come to love it all, and to know something of the divine love. People are not very poetic today. That is one reason for our spiritual dryness – 'When I try to pray, I just dry up,' is something we often hear. A daily dose of the Psalms is like rain on dry land.

It is important to remember that at this stage not any Psalm will do. Some will not fit, like the wrong shoe. We could start by sticking to our favourites. There are 150 to choose from.

Part of the secret of the Psalms is their rhythm. Rhythm is one of the strongest elements in music. The powerful rhythms of the pop group, or the lilting rhythm of a waltz, affect us deeply. The rhythm of the poetry in psalms quietens down our frazzled and un-quiet minds. Saying a psalm aloud, but very gently and slowly, we find this seems to open up our pores, our spirit begins to breathe. Slowly, slowly, thoughtfully, gently – lightly and never stodgily. 'I've got rhythm' is, in a way, a part of the gospel. The prayer of the Church is full of 'hymns and psalms and spiritual songs' (Colossians 3.16). Music and poetry are LIFE, living life and enjoying it, and living it to the depths of our being.

The possibilities are endless, but the lesson is profound. We need something to do. This is especially true of males, who would go to church in far larger numbers if they all had something to do instead of just sitting in a pew, for men (in our culture at least) can tend to be uncomfortable with doing sensitive things in a group, but they can jump at something practical to do.

I have said that God is not gas, nor a ghost. It might seem as though this were saying that silent, private prayer was not the right thing to be doing. In fact, the opposite is true. All we have been doing is putting the balance right. We go about things in the wrong way, in a way which is not natural. It is not that one approach is right, another wrong. Rather it is that we have overdone quiet, private prayer, so that the other approach has been forgotten. That needs to be put right.

Now that we have said all that, we can go back to our old idea of private prayer and see it in a new light. It is not always appropriate or desirable to worship with pictures and candles and things to do. Sometimes they get in the way. There are times when prayer in privacy and in silence is the only way. We find this in everyday life. There have been people who have known each other for many years and yet have never met. You find this not just with pen-friends but with very great friendships which have been struck up and maintained entirely through the post or by telephone. I know someone who was taught by a very great expert, through correspondence and occasional telephone calls. They became very great friends, and it was a tragedy that after twenty-five years, just as the pupil gained for the first time an opportunity to come to England, the teacher died. Right to the end that friendship was similar to the practice of silent prayer. Deprived of sight and touch, it thrived through the post.

Prayer can be like that, and yet, just as the pupil hoped to meet her teacher, so for us private prayer can never be enough, for we want to meet God in the flesh, as it were. All our private prayer needs a solid foundation in the scriptures, in the Church and in the sacraments. Some people are indeed called to quiet, private prayer in a big way. For example, for some monks and nuns much of their prayer may be in solitude and silence. Such silent prayer is being discovered by many people today, both in prayer groups and by taking part in retreats, and visiting religious communities. But it is a mistake to keep attempting to make it a big thing if it isn't for us.

Listening to God in the silence is a story all on its own, and there is no room to go into it here, nor is there any need, as there are plenty of books about it already. It is one of God's great gifts. But we need to start where we are. Concentrating hard isn't how we usually get on with our family – it's more down-to-earth and practical than that.

We are human, and that is how God made us. He has a way of deepening us as we go along, but in the meantime what we really want is to see, to touch, to do.

✄

1 Psalms 23 and 84 are from *Celebrating Common Prayer* (Mowbray 1992). Copyright © The European Province of the Society of Saint Francis 1992.

9 Day in, day out

The quest for how we might pray goes on. We have discovered some things already, but there is yet more. If we return to our average family (if there is such a thing) and ask the question, 'How often do its members normally see each other?' the answer would usually be, 'every day'. Certainly for a husband and wife that would be normal (work and circumstances permitting). The New Testament speaks of our relationship with God as being like that of bride and bridegroom, nothing less. This implies that prayer which is worth its salt will happen every day. There is something to be discovered here which is a bit surprising.

The story begins with Jesus. He prayed first of all by going to the temple and the synagogue and joining in the services. Then there were also the set prayers which all devout Jews said at least three times each day. Everybody said them and, even when they were alone, they had a tremendous sense that all of them, a whole people, were praying together. Usually the prayers would be said in the family.

In addition to all of this, Jesus sometimes went off into the fields to pray alone. We find the same thing with the apostles in the Book of Acts: at least three prayer-times, at the third, sixth, and ninth hours (morning, midday, and afternoon – see Acts 2.15, 10.9, and 10.30). Prayer in such a culture was usually patterned, offered at particular times each day, and was done together in the home, or wherever you happened to be. On one occasion St Peter chose the roof of a house (Acts 10.9). One very important thing about it would have been the sense of togetherness, even if you were alone. It was prayer with a sense of belonging, and often it used music and singing, and going to special places set apart for the purpose (the temple and the synagogue).

You might want to query this – didn't Jesus say we were to pray in secret with the door shut? He did indeed, but he was being mischievous, almost sarcastic. Palestinian houses only had one room, and everyone was in it together. The only part with a door was the pantry, and Jesus was gently mocking the way some people paraded their piety in the streets, telling them, with a sense of humour, to pray in the pantry, where no one would see them (Matthew 6.6). It is on a par with other leg-pulls, as in the place where he compares God to a burglar and a thief (Matthew 24.43). Elsewhere in St Matthew's gospel, we read that it is 'where two or three are gathered together in my name that I am in the midst of them' (18.20). So Matthew too was familiar with the togetherness of Christian prayer.

That is the kind of thing we read in the New Testament. How did it continue after that? Once we reach the years after New Testament times, we begin to find more information about how Christians prayed. They did it at least three times a day, sometimes as much as seven or eight. Jesus had, after all, said we should 'pray always' (Luke 18.1), and Paul tells us to 'pray without ceasing' (1 Thessalonians 5.17). The more often our kettle is brought to the fire, the more likely it is to stay on the boil. There were set prayers; sometimes they sang psalms and hymns, and read passages of scripture, and there were simple ceremonies as well.

In particular they had a ceremony to mark lighting-up time. In times before electricity it was necessary, when dusk had come, to light the lamps in the house, and in a rich family's large house this could mean going from room to room, leaving lamps burning at strategic points. In the town, lanterns would have been hung out in the street. It was a very old custom to pray at this moment, and for the early Christians lighting-up time became one of the most important moments in the day. They saw the living flame as being the light of Christ shining in the darkness. Darkness is chased away from homes, hearts and minds, as the lamps are lit with hymn-singing and prayers in honour of Jesus the Lord. This prayer of the lamplighting became extremely popular, and we hear of it in all kinds of far-flung places, not least in the British

Isles. Not many years ago a hoard of ancient Roman church plate was dug up in a field at Water Newton. Amongst the bowls and vases were many fragments of precious, beautiful lamps.

The custom of the lamplighting had very soon passed from the home into the church. From the fourth century onwards we begin to see how Christians prayed, and it is clear that they enjoyed their religion. They went to church twice a day. In the morning there was a short service which lasted about half an hour. It consisted of hymn-singing, including psalms, and then at the end there were prayers for the needs of the world, very similar to the intercessions we have in our churches today. In the evening there was a similar service, but this time it started with the lighting of the lamps. And how they enjoyed it!

First of all they gathered in the twilight. Then someone came in with a lamp (or a candle) and they began to sing, of Christ and his light. They lit as many lamps as they could, hundreds of them, suspended from the ceiling, winking flames from wicks floating in olive oil. In many places they sang this very ancient hymn:

> O joyful light,
>   from the pure glory of the eternal Father,
> O holy, blessed Jesus Christ.
>
> As we come to the setting of the sun
> and see the evening light,
> We give thanks and praise to the Father and to the Son
> and to the Holy Spirit of God . . .[1]

The service was full of singing, a kind of ancient *Songs of Praise*. It was very colourful, with processions, the sweet aromas of incense (which is really an ancient form of aerosol), and the full use of beautiful buildings. This was prayer! This was how they prayed. Then they went off and prayed at their meal-tables and before going to bed, and in the middle of their daily work, encouraged and inspired by the daily round of beautiful services.

There was a tremendous sense of belonging, so much so that, even when people were prevented from getting to church, they prayed wherever they were, at the same time as the service was going on, adding their contribution from a distance.

For many centuries, this is how Christians prayed. It was all profoundly rooted in the church. Prayer is God's take-away gift. People found it with their fellow Christians in church, and then took it away and kept it going through the rest of the day and night. They returned to prayer as we return to a bunch of flowers to sniff them. That is how Christian prayer used to be. And it was like that for a long, long time, right up to the present day in some parts of the world.

Still today in Syria and Iraq, Christians go to their churches every day for services which are full of participation and singing. If they can not get to church, they imitate parts of the service simply where they are. So shepherds, when they pray, do it at the times when the service is going on in church, every morning and evening. They mark a cross on a wall or tree, and repeat a few phrases from the service, such as, 'Make me a pure heart, O God.' They say the Lord's Prayer and the 'Holy, Holy, Holy', and then they make a profound bow and sign themselves with the sign of the life-giving cross. They know they are not alone. They are praying, even though at a distance, with their people. The Syrian countryside must be strewn with these roughly-scratched crosses.

What happened to the daily services? They were still being kept up not so long ago. If you had been alive at the time of Long John Silver and three-cornered hats, your local parish church would very likely have had two services every day which were well attended. In eighteenth-century London some churches were so well attended that they had to have four services every day of the week. St James's Piccadilly, in London, was such a church. However, even then, the services were not what they had been in ancient times. They were rather dull, and very wordy – a far cry from the enjoyable lighting of lamps. The main problem was that, over the years, a division grew up between clergy and people, so that these daily services were taken over in effect by the clergy, and the people no longer had much to do. So in most parts of the world they lost interest and stopped coming. And as a result prayer gradually became more of a struggle. In the end the only people to feel completely at home in church were the clergy.

The tradition of the daily services has never entirely disappeared. It still survives in our cathedrals and in many parishes. But in the parishes it is hardly recognizable.

Imagine you are walking by a church and decide to go in. The church is empty. Before you is a sea of pews. You look up and see, at the front, a priest. He is praying with a book. You sit there and rest your feet for a bit. At certain points the priest gets up, or kneels or sits. 'What is he doing?' you think. He is in fact doing something which all clergy in the Church of England and in other churches are bound to do every day. In the Church of England the clergy should ring the bell before they do it, both morning and evening. There are some clergy nowadays who no longer bother, but the obligation to do it every day is clearly laid out in their job-description.

What is this strange activity which so many people have never heard of, but which is well known to every single priest and deacon, and to the ministers of other churches, even if they don't always do it?

It is commonly called the 'Daily Office'. It is none other than the daily service of psalms and prayers we have been describing, but now performed largely in private by the clergy, sometimes together with some lay folk. The morning and evening services are called Mattins and Evensong in the Church of England, while in the Roman Catholic Church their traditional name is Lauds and Vespers. Often we just call them Morning and Evening Prayer. We may be familiar with Evensong on a Sunday evening, when it is sung with hymns. But Evensong goes on every day of the week. In our English cathedrals there is usually a choir for it, every single day.

When the parish clergy say it on their own, it may be a shrivelled old plant compared with what it was, but most clergy who use it will be quick to tell you how important and helpful it is for them, not least because it gives a sense of praying with the whole Church, a sense of not being alone in prayer, but of belonging.

This very simplified historical sketch has led us to a curiosity. It has something to tell us about our problems in finding God, funnily enough, and we need next to see what exactly that might be.

1 *Celebrating Common Prayer* (Mowbray 1992), p. 229. Copyright © The European Province of the Society of Saint Francis 1992.

10 *Doing it ourselves*

We saw in the last chapter that in the past, daily prayer for Christians was very different from our usual idea of what prayer is. Maybe we need to rediscover it today. In fact this is now happening in more and more places. It is something that is catching on in a big way. One of these places is an ordinary parish in the north of England, where there has been a real attempt to enable the daily prayer to become the prayer of the people. In this parish, the priest found it increasingly difficult to say the daily office on his own – it often seemed too dry and formal. Now, after a few years of experiment, all of that has changed.

Twice a day people gather in a side chapel specially fitted out for the purpose. It is small, intimate and uncluttered, and the service is simplicity itself, and lasts about twenty-five minutes. And while it follows a set form, there is also a homely spontaneity about it.

When it is time to start, whoever is leading the service (it is not always the vicar) begins the singing of a refrain, and at the evening service they have the lighting of the lamps, beginning with the lighting of a large candle.

Then all sit to listen. Someone takes the psalter and reads out a psalm, very slowly and quietly, as a gentle meditation. This is followed by a time of silence. Then all listen to the psalm-prayer.

Next they sing a canticle. Another silence. Another prayer.

Then a short reading and a hymn.

The last part of the service is made up of informal prayer and intercession, where people can chip in with things they wish to pray for.

It then ends with the Our Father and a prayer.

This cannot give you an idea of the atmosphere. Just to describe a service like that is like asking what Fred looks like, and being shown his x-ray. The important thing is the atmosphere and feel of the service, and that cannot be described. Here, however, are some comments by a parishioner:

> At present, after nearly four years' use and the second set of Office Books, necessitated by wear and tear, there has been rarely a day on which there have been less than three people present at Daily Prayer – even when the Vicar has been away from the parish. The attendances vary, but there are generally between three and ten with sometimes more, especially on the Saturday evening, when we do it with a bit more beauty and music . . . During the week there are upwards of twenty-five separate individuals who attend the

office . . . The 'Office Book' is also noticeable in the homes of parishioners and many of the sick and housebound have commented on the feeling of being strengthened by the sense of taking an active part in the prayer-life of the church. It is not uncommon for the Office Book to be taken along when people have to go into hospital. Several families, five at the last count, make a regular point of meeting together to pray the Office, usually gathering at the home of a relative who because of reasons of age and infirmity cannot get to church. The best, most recent estimate of numbers of people who regularly use the Office at home is upwards of sixty. The Daily Office of the Church has become loved and cherished again. The people have taken it to their hearts and it has filled a need which wasn't initially perceived to be there. As one parishioner said to the Vicar, 'Ee, Vicar, it has changed my life.' . . . It has not only had a positive effect on the life of individuals but it has also had a strengthening effect on the overall corporate, caring worship of the parish.[1]

This way of doing daily prayer (and it really is 'doing' it) is one of the gifts God offers to his Church. It is because we have almost lost it, that many of our present problems have arisen. It is now being rediscovered by Christians all over the world. In Africa, America, France, Germany, Italy, and many other places, there are now churches here and there where people come day by day to the office. And it is particularly successful in places where it is offered with a bit of music, a bit of visual beauty, some actions to participate in, and a strong sense of belonging, and a sense of doing it with the universal Church. It proves that all we have learnt in this book about comparing prayer with our daily behaviour is on the right lines. This way of prayer called the 'daily office' is an answer to the question, 'What must I do?' It gives us something clear and identifiable to do. It is patterned, following familiar ways – just as when we greet each other in the street. It gives us regularity, order and rhythm. It allows us to relax, and let ourselves be carried along, even though our mind may be wandering some of the time. It pickles us in the life-giving story whose centre is Jesus. It keeps us remembering, not allowing us to forget. It warms us up, not letting us go cold. We give ourselves to it, we commit ourselves, just as we do in taking on a full-time job, and, just like a job, it requires of us a certain amount of obedience and loyalty. It is a real apprenticeship.

This way of prayer gives us set forms so that we know where we stand. We have a clear idea of what we need to do, while at the same time we can discover the freedom to be relaxed and spontaneous in the doing of it. It is more than empty convention – it pays big dividends. To be sure, it does not pay them as we would like them, every day on demand. The commitment requires that we wait for them. The dividends of daily prayer are big, and they come in the long term, over the years. When we are faithful to God, he is faithful to us.

At the same time the words remind us that of ourselves we can do nothing. Only God can make it work. We can't – not on our own, anyway. We water the plant, says St Paul, but God gives the growth (1 Corinthians 3.6). The daily office helps us to persevere (Romans 12.12), it helps us to have a sense that God is with us all the time. It also helps us to realize that we are not alone. It is not just my private prayer (although it is that too). It is the prayer of the Church, in which we are all taken up together by the Holy Spirit, as if we were stepping on an escalator.

It instils in us a tremendous sense of praying together with people in all the world, and with the saints who stand before the throne of God. And when we get into its rhythm we begin to find we are, as it were, dancing with the Trinity. Christ prays in us, we pray in him, the Holy Spirit takes us in the flow, up to the love of the Father, and then it all goes with us, into our front room, into the street, the bus, the newsagent's, wherever life takes us in its daily round.

We are not able to describe the best things in life. We simply have to get people to try them, to see for themselves. You may think of all kinds of objections. In particular, you will probably be saying that you can't go to church twice a day – it's impossible. Your work hours are wrong, or you can't leave the family, and so on. But the point is this: let those who can, those who are free, go to church to pray with their clergy (or without, if there are none). Then let everyone else do what they can. Try and say a prayer wherever you are, at the time they are praying in church. There may be at least one day in the week when you can make time to go to one of the services. Let that keep your private prayers going each day for the rest of the week. See what you can do to get together with other people to offer now and again the Church's prayers.

And remember that we can't just sit down and read through some words. We must find some ways of savouring them, and ways of creating an atmosphere for prayer. Turn the lights down (that helps us to relax with others and to be open to God, to let Him in), have a candle, a picture, something like that. And sing something, even if it is only very simple, such as one verse of 'The day thou gavest'.

There is still another question: why should it be necessary to pray every day? Isn't it enough to pray on Sunday? The trouble is that by the time Monday morning comes, Sunday seems a long way away. It is like hoovering the carpet, or combing our hair – twenty-four hours later the carpet or the hair is in a mess again. It will take a long time for an onion to get pickled if we only put it in vinegar for one hour every Sunday: it needs to stay in all the time. In our search for the taste of God, we need to stay at it all the time. In practice this has meant that Christians have prayed to God every day, and not just on Sundays.

Jesus, as a devout Jew, would have prayed every morning and every evening. It isn't something you can do just now and again, when you feel like it. It hasn't got rhythm then. When you pray, have you got rhythm? If you haven't, then you are trying to do it in an unnatural way. Our daily lives are full of rhythm – getting up, washing, breakfast, catching the bus; then the day's work with its breaks for rest and refreshment, then the predictable patterns of the evening, and finally we go to bed. If these things did not follow a regular pattern we should go out of our mind.

It is hardly surprising therefore that people find prayer to be a dead loss when they don't do it rhythmically. They are trying to do something unnatural.

You might raise an objection here. Surely, you may say, isn't it a normal part of daily life to do some things spontaneously? Like visiting friends, or going to the pub? We don't usually do that in a fixed daily pattern. Here, however, we have touched on the heart of the matter. God is not interested in simply being an acquaintance. The New Testament puts it very differently from that, for it says that we and God are bride and bridegroom. The bridegroom gave his life for his spouse, the Church – which is us. You don't go through all of that just to have people as occasional acquaintances! The Bible takes us back again and again to the model of marriage. And here is a very ancient lesson which each generation has to learn again for itself. Occasional outings are for fun: marriage is for real. And we know what that means. It means staying with the daily round through thick and thin. There will be good times and bad, enjoyable times and boring ones. Prayer and family life are the same. You can't miss your morning prayers because you don't feel like it. You can't give up if you are going through a bad patch. You don't pass a neighbour in the street without talking, just because today you aren't in the mood. Why treat God like that, and expect to get away with it?

Time and again we find that we learn about God from how we live our daily lives, whether it is out and about, or at home in the family. Both in life and in prayer the bad patches are just as important for our growth as the good ones.

So there we are. Not much more can be said about daily prayer in a book. People won't be convinced until they try it. And it needs to be a local Christian community that tries it, rather than just some private groups. Day in, day out, we pursue our quest for God, and he acts within us, empowering our quest, and granting us bit by bit that impossible thing – a glimpse of God. 'Blessed are the pure in heart: they shall see God.'

1 A. Briscoe, 'The Haydock Office', *CR Quarterly* 353 (Mirfield 1991), pp. 6ff.

11 *The greatest prayer*

How can we get to know God? That has been our question all the way through this book. We have been discovering a few things which don't always occur to us, and we have done it using insights from our own daily life and come-and-go with other people. There is too much to be said in a small book such as this, but the picture would be seriously lacking if we did not include one more thing before we finish. Again, it may come as something rather unexpected.

If prayer is partly about set patterns, is there one prayer which ranks amongst the greatest? There is such a prayer, and it stands out from all the others. It is a good question whether even the Lord's Prayer is as great as this one. It is a very strange fact that clergy don't often teach people about this prayer, and yet there can be little doubt that it lies near the heart of the Christian life. I suppose the reason is that we don't often talk about the things which are most important in our life – like breath, for instance. They are so familiar that it doesn't occur to us to draw attention to them. But this prayer is so great and so fundamental to us that it isn't enough that its importance should be known only to the clergy. The fact that certain important things are familiar to the clergy but not to lay folk is one reason why many Christians are 'up a gum-tree' – it is time now to come down, to come home, and look at what is one of the greatest prayers of all.

We are told in the New Testament that at the Last Supper Jesus took bread and wine; he gave thanks over them, broke the bread, and distributed them to those at table (Luke 22.14–20). The New Testament tells us nothing about what Jesus said in his 'thanks'. It just says, 'He gave thanks.' What words did he use? In fact, we know roughly what they would have been. At the time of Jesus in Palestine there was a special grace which was said over the bread and the wine. It could begin something like this:

> *Host:* Let us give thanks to the Lord our God
> *All:* It is right to give him thanks and praise.

The father of the family then blessed God for all the good things God had done for his people. If you are used to attending the eucharist (communion, or mass) you will immediately recognize this. It is a prayer which is at the centre of the eucharist. It has many names. It is often called the Eucharistic Prayer, or the Great Thanksgiving. It is also referred to by other names. This Great Prayer starts with 'Let us give thanks . . .', it goes on to the 'Holy, holy, holy', on again to the story of the Last Supper, and the acclamation 'Christ has died, Christ is risen, Christ will come again', and then on again until we all say 'Amen'.

It is a long prayer, the longest in the service. And the amazing thing about it is that it has been given to us by the memory of the Church. This is a very special prayer indeed. It has been handed on from generation to generation like an heirloom, starting with the Last Supper, or even before it, in the meals Jesus often had with his disciples. People have treasured it with their lives, and carefully handed it on from the Last Supper, Sunday by Sunday, in the Church's worship.

If we want to know why we use it, we need to go through it, having its various parts explained. I will try and do this in a simple way.

Jesus took the bread and the wine and gave thanks to God for all the things God has done for his people. There is a type of Jewish prayer found in many places in the Old and New Testaments which will have been in Jesus and his disciples' bones. Such a prayer starts by blessing God or giving thanks to him. Then it lists all the things he has done for us (look, for example, at Daniel 2.20–23; Psalm 103; Ephesians 1.3–14; Luke 1.68–79; 1 Peter 1.3–5).

This listing of God's wonderful deeds is a very biblical way of praying. When people said a grace at table they also prayed in this way. And it is such a prayer that Jesus will have used when he 'gave thanks'. In the eucharistic prayer we continue to do this. We thank the Father for all the things he has done for us in Jesus: his birth, his passion and death, and his resurrection. There is a great list of all we have received from God. So this prayer gives thanks too for all God's gifts to us in creating the world.

After that, we all sing, 'Holy, holy, holy'. This hymn is very old indeed, and is used in the Sabbath service in the synagogue today. We share it with the Jews. It gives us the picture of all created things on earth and in heaven praising God.

Then, on we go with the story of the Last Supper: 'He took bread, gave you thanks and broke it, and said, This is my body which is given for you . . .' and so on. These words used to be said at the time of receiving communion, but they came to be included inside the great prayer. They make it clear that here we are not dealing with mere symbolism. We are dealing with something powerfully real – the astonishing words of Jesus: 'This is my body . . . This is my blood.' Queen Elizabeth I composed a short poem about this which puts it in a nutshell:

> 'Twas God the word that spake it,
> He took the Bread and brake it,
> And what that word did make it
> That I believe, and take it.

When this Last Supper account is finished, we all say the acclamation: 'Christ has died, Christ is risen, Christ will come again', or something similar.

Why do we all have to say this at this point? Jesus said, 'Do this in remembrance of me.' He didn't mean 'remembering' as thinking about something dead and gone. Our word 'remember' is not a very good one for what Jesus meant. He used a word in his language which does not mean simply 'remember', it means something like 're-live'. It means thinking of something in such a way that it is not just a memory, but becomes present. He meant that in our remembering we shall be there at his cross and his rising again. It will be real. And it will change us. So, when we all say, 'Christ has died, Christ is risen, Christ will come again,' we are obeying, doing what Jesus told us to do – 'Do this in remembrance of me.'

Like many characters in the New Testament we ask, 'What must I do?' Jesus' message was not simply about believing – it was also about responding to our natural question: 'What must I do?' Here is one of his answers: 'Do this.' Do this in memory of me. Those were his words.

After this, the prayer goes on again. If anything is worth doing, it is worth doing twice, and so the prayer now repeats what we have just said: 'And so, Father, remembering his death upon the cross, his resurrection from the dead, and his ascension into heaven, we bring before you this bread and this cup . . .'

The Jews remember here in this part of the prayer the way God rescued his people from Egypt and led them into the promised land. We (the Church) changed the words, so that instead we remember God rescuing us through Jesus, in his death and resurrection and all that was done in him for us. This prayer is a 'thank you', which is what the word 'grace' means.

But notice it doesn't stop at remembering. It goes on to offer to God the gifts of Christ's body and blood: 'We bring before you this bread and this cup.' What does this mean? Surely God does not want us to offer the body of Jesus to him as the Jews used to sacrifice animals in the temple? Here we come to something which is at the heart of the Christian life. It is Christ who does the giving. We have nothing to give, for we have received it all from God in the first place. Yet, with a generosity beyond our comprehending, Christ says, 'Come on, do it with me. Let us offer together.' So we step with him on to his escalator of prayer (remember Jacob's ladder in Genesis 28.12).

Christ gives himself to the Father. We offer, he offers, we are offered, he is offered – quite a riddle!

That is a good word for it, for the riddle is this: we never pray on our own. We may pray to Christ, but he also prays in us. It is not just our private effort. And we pray in him, for we are in the Body of Christ. You may think this is gobbledygook, all riddles. In a sense that is just what it is; so great is the mystery, that it is impossible to put it into words that make sense. As with many of the deep things in life, we have to use riddles to talk about it. That is why this ancient prayer ends with words which are like a riddle:

> Through him, and with him, and in him,
> In the power of the Holy Spirit.
> (see Romans 11.36)

Behind all this riddle lies something very simple. Wherever there is love, there will be giving, there will be gifts. That is what love is about. Christ offers everything

– his incarnation, his earthly life, his passion, his cross and burial, his resurrection and ascension. Nothing less than all of it is held before God in this service over which Christ presides. And it is set forth by him in our presenting of the bread and wine.

Now the prayer goes on to the next thing. It asks God to send his Holy Spirit on us and on the bread and wine; to send the One who will lead us into all truth. 'Send your Holy Spirit on us your people . . .' Sometimes here there are intercessions, prayers for the Church on earth and in heaven. And then in its last few words the prayer scatters words of praise like confetti.

Finally comes the 'Amen'. Unfortunately, we often mumble it. St Augustine said that this Amen was the people's signature to the Great Thanksgiving, and it should ring out through the Church. 'Amen,' we say: 'So be it!' – just as they would have done at the Last Supper.

What a long prayer, the Eucharistic Prayer, how full of words! Yet it is one of the greatest prayers we can ever say. It has been passed down to us from the Last Supper, unchanged in its essentials. And it has been passed on to us by the Church, by Christians meeting faithfully Sunday by Sunday, to break the bread and so share in the mystery of Christ's generosity.

There are many versions of this prayer. Just as with hymns, people from earliest times have composed their own versions. One of the oldest is now in the Alternative Service Book Rite A, in its Third Eucharistic Prayer (Roman Catholic Prayer 2, Methodist B12), although it is somewhat adapted. This is very, very old indeed, going back to about the year 150, that is, within living memory of the apostles. St John, for instance, had died only about fifty years before. It is an amazing contact with the first Christians.

What has all of this to do with the newsagent's? What has it to do with our desire to find God? It has everything to do with these things. Many people go to church looking for a special experience. Some people get one, and it is very good when that happens. But having experiences is not the important thing. That way many people would be disappointed for much of the time. If you think of your own family, you will know that family life is not all special experiences – the basic thing about family life is the ordinary story which unfolds from day to day. Christian worship is like that. It is not so much about having a 'trip'. Rather is it about entering into a story. The great Eucharistic Prayer recounts the story, the story of Jesus and of God's way with us, with and through Jesus.

It is a saving story because it is alive. Not like the story of Robin Hood, who is dead and gone, but like our own story and our own memories about ourselves, which still live in us. Every person is full of vivid memories, some pleasant, some unpleasant. Some of them are very much alive for us – when we sit and think of some people and events we have known, it is as if we were there.

The eucharist is even more powerful than our memories. In it the things remembered, the birth and life of Christ, his cross, death and resurrection, are a dynamic presence. So he himself is present in various ways in the eucharist. Physically present in the bread and wine. Present also in the Word which we hear, and which has power to save and create anew. Present also, as the eucharistic prayer says, in all the people present – we see him in each other.

We may not always 'feel' this presence. Just as in family life, it doesn't keep sweeping you off your feet with special experiences: it bears fruit over a long time. We gradually become steeped in the living story of Jesus, just as onions slowly become pickled.

So here we are. Just like the Lord on the night on which he was betrayed, we take bread and wine, we give thanks (in the great Eucharistic Prayer), we break the bread, and then we take it all in: we receive communion. When the young man asked Jesus, 'What must I do?' (Mark 10.17), Jesus told him to follow him, to come and be with him, in his presence. So at the holy table we ask, 'What can I do?', and Christ tells us, 'Do this in memory of me.' In other words, 'Do this and I will be present. Then follow me.'

12 *Where we started*

Where is God? That is what we asked at the beginning. We treated it like a thread, pulling on it to see what it unravelled. It is my hope that you have discovered something as a result. This 'something' is not likely to be a magic answer to all your problems. It won't put everything right just like that. But if we Christians take this 'something' seriously and start acting upon it, it will set us on the way, equipping us for our quest for God.

The Christian Church is like a very old plant. People have forgotten how to look after it, and its leaves have become a bit brown at the edges. This plant needs its leaves nourishing. In other words, the Church, which is green in some parts and slightly wilting in others, depends on us, who are people who need to rediscover how to pray – how to pray not just with words, but through sight, sound, and touch. We need to rediscover the unity of God's plant the Church, for we never pray alone, but as members of Christ's body. One thing we need to rediscover is a special kind of worship, joining those many people today who are rediscovering the Daily Office.

Other bits of repair work have already been done, such as improvements in the Sunday services and in people's participation. But there is still much to be done in getting the heart of it right.

It begins with the Lord's Supper on Sundays. When we remember, we relive the drama through which we have been saved, we join in Christ's offering, we receive his gifts, and through it God works to make of us a single people, the Body of Christ.

Then this thread continues through the ordinary weekdays, not least with the Church's daily prayer. What happens on Sundays then doesn't go cold, but is spread out through the week.

Then we take it, like ingredients for a cake, and mix it in with the flour of daily life – the queue for the *Daily Mirror*, Mars bars and packets of Silk Cut. All the moments, both special and ordinary, of every day.

Those moments will now change slightly. The reason for this is that in the worship we meet a Christ who changes us. Then we begin to recognize him everywhere in the ordinary world. Worship has the power to carry out an impossible transformation – so that we may become bigger-hearted, more generous, more open-eyed about the holiness of God's world. What we meet in church is all around us. All we need is to have our eyes opened.

God is there in the newsagent's. He is all around us and in us. There is tremendous good sense and generosity in other people. This is always a sign of the presence of Christ. Our modern society, for all its faults, is full of signs of Christ. It respects persons and their dignity and their rights in a way which our grandparents could not have dreamed of. It fails very badly in many ways, but is still a more caring society than we have ever had. We can go into hospital and be cared for by our fellow human beings, where for our great-grandparents there would have been no hospital. People raise amazing amounts of money for the starving in Africa, where a few years ago nobody bothered. Such goodness is always a sign of the presence of Christ. If we are looking for God, then the Church's worship opens our eyes, so that we begin to be able to see him in the people we meet every day.

If we start there, by looking for the signs of God in all that is good, then we can go on to face fairly and squarely all that is bad. No one can be under any illusion about the state of the world we live in. The things we see on television can be almost impossible for us to take. And there is so much human suffering and indignity that we turn a blind eye to. These people are in countries too far away for it to be our affair!

And then apart from all the violence and evil, the ordinary failings of everyday folk get no better either – human pettiness is as bad as ever it was. Looking after number one, dishonesty at work, gossip and bad feeling – all of these are as old as humankind itself. Sin is ingrained in us.

God is to be found in all of the evil, as well as in the good things. He speaks in our conscience, and is the voice calling us to love for our neighbour, to right living, and to reverence for the world God has created.

We don't know what it is to be good. We have so much to learn about it. And yet we see in the scriptures a Christ who believes that we can all become better and more noble than we are. He is not past and gone – we meet him in daily life.

His presence is there in our neighbours, in all their need and suffering, their troubles and worries, and he is there in all the pleasure and goodness we find in them. In supporting them we are supporting Him. 'As often as you did it to the least of these, you did it to me' (Matthew 25.40). The worship of the Church is a school in all of this.

Where is God? He is all around us. Worship will show us how to recognize him. Daily prayer, day in, day out, will 'pickle' us in something new. In prayer and worship we taste God 'neat'. When we have received that strong taste of him 'neat', we find we are able to taste the same flavour in the people and things of everyday life.

Come, then, 'to Mount Zion, to the city of the living God, the heavenly Jerusalem, and to innumerable angels in festal gathering, and to the assembly of the first-born who are enrolled in heaven, and to a judge who is God of all, and to the spirit of the just made perfect, and to Jesus, the mediator of the new covenant'[1]. Come and discover him. For in discovering him, we find ourselves.

---

1   Hebrews 12.22–4 (RSV).

What Next?

Here are two suggestions for daily prayer. The first is a book called *Celebrating Common Prayer* (Mowbray 1992). On pages 281 to 283 you will find a simple explanation of the forms of prayer which come after (on pages 284 to 324). You will also find in other parts of the book many things to help in saying our prayers.

Another possibility is three little books by Jim Cotter: *Prayer in the Morning, Prayer in the Day*, and *Prayer at Night* (Cairns Publications 1988, 1989).

A Prayer Stool

Many people today use a prayer stool to pray. It makes it possible for you to kneel for long periods, if necessary, without any discomfort. One can be made simply by nailing three pieces of wood together. More sophisticated prayer stools have hinged supports, so they can be folded away, and perhaps a slightly sloping top.

Kneel on the ground, put the stool over your heels, and sit back.

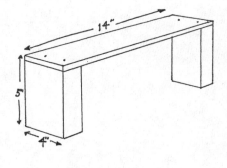

Approximate measurements for making a prayer stool.

Also published by

Tri∧ngle

The PRAYING WITH series
A series of books making accessible the words of some of the
great characters and traditions of faith for use by all
Christians.
There are 14 titles in the series, including:

PRAYING WITH SAINT AUGUSTINE
Introduction by Murray Watts

PRAYING WITH SAINT FRANCIS
Introduction by David Ford

PRAYING WITH HIGHLAND CHRISTIANS
Introduction by Sally Magnusson

PRAYING WITH THE NEW TESTAMENT
Introduction by Joyce Huggett

PRAYING WITH SAINT TERESA
Introduction by Elaine Storkey

PRAYING WITH THE JEWISH TRADITION
Introduction by Lionel Blue

PRAYING WITH THE OLD TESTAMENT
Introduction by Richard Holloway

PRAYING WITH THE ORTHODOX TRADITION
Preface by Kallistos Ware

PRAYING WITH THE ENGLISH HYMN WRITERS
Compiled and Introduced by Timothy Dudley-Smith

PRAYING WITH THE ENGLISH MYSTICS
Compiled and Introduced by Jenny Robertson

PRAYING WITH THE ENGLISH TRADITION
Compiled by Margaret Pawley
Preface by Robert Runcie

PRAYING WITH THE ENGLISH POETS
Compiled and Introduced by Ruth Etchells

PRAYING WITH THE MARTYRS
Preface by Madeleine L'Engle

PRAYING WITH JOHN DONNE AND GEORGE
HERBERT
Preface by Richard Harries

Books by
DAVID ADAM

THE EDGE OF GLORY
Prayers in the Celtic tradition

Modern prayers which recapture the Celtic way of
intertwining divine glory with the ordinariness of
everyday events.

THE CRY OF THE DEER
Meditations on the Hymn of St Patrick

Meditations leading to practical exercises which take us
deeper in to the prayer experience in affirming the Presence
of God.

TIDES AND SEASONS
Modern prayers in the Celtic tradition

A series of prayers which echo the rhythms of creation,
finding their parallels in our spiritual lives and in the highs
and lows of all human experience.

THE EYE OF THE EAGLE
Meditations on the hymn 'Be thou my vision'

David Adam takes us through the words of the Celtic hymn,
'Be thou my vision', discovering the spiritual riches that are
hidden in all our lives.

POWER LINES
Celtic prayers about work

A series of modern prayers about work which incorporate the insights of the Celtic tradition. The book opens up Celtic patterns of prayer to focus on the work we all do in the presence of God.

BORDER LANDS
The Best of David Adam

An SPCK hardback edition of selections from the first four of David Adam's books – an ideal introduction to Celtic spirituality.

More books from

THE VOICE FROM THE CROSS
by Donald Coggan

In a series of striking meditations on Jesus' seven last words
from the cross, the former Archbishop of Canterbury
challenges us all to look more deeply into the central events
for the Christian faith.

SAINTS ALIVE!
Biblical Reflections on the Lives of the Saints
by Michael Marshall

Saints Alive! offers a six-week series of daily meditations
providing Bible readings and reflections on the way
particular saints have lived out biblical principles and ideas.

THE TRUTH ABOUT LOVE
Re-introducing the Good News
by William Countryman

A remarkably fresh presentation of the message of Jesus,
written with a pastoral concern for all Christians. William
Countryman challenges us all to find the authentic good
news and live abundantly in faith, hope and love.

PATHS OF THE HEART
Prayers of Medieval Christians
edited by John Blakesley
Foreword by Brother Ramon SSF

A collection of moving and inspiring prayers to enrich
Christian devotional lives by their imaginative and
perceptive spirituality

Triangle and SPCK Books
can be obtained from
all good bookshops.
In case of difficulty,
or for a complete list of all our books,
contact:
SPCK Mail Order
36 Steep Hill
Lincoln
LN2 1LU
(tel: 0522 527 486)